VAISHNO DEVI

The Powerful Goddess

First Published in 2024 by

Om KIDZ | Om Books International

Corporate & Editorial Office
A-12, Sector 64, Noida 201 301
Uttar Pradesh, India
Phone: +91 120 477 4100
Email: editorial@ombooks.com
Website: www.ombooksinternational.com

Sales Office
107, Ansari Road, Darya Ganj
New Delhi 110 002, India
Phone: +91 11 4000 9000
Email: sales@ombooks.com

ISBN: 978-81-19749-40-9

Printed in India

10 9 8 7 6 5 4 3 2 1

VAISHNO DEVI
The Powerful Goddess

Om KIDZ
An imprint of Om Books International

Long long ago, when the Earth was full of demons, the holy goddess—also known as Shakti—was busy destroying them. One day, her three forms—Maha Kali, Maha Lakshmi and Maha Saraswati—became one. A bright light flashed across the heavens. From the light emerged a beautiful divine girl.

"Oh Holy Mothers! What is the purpose of my creation?" asked the little girl. "We want you to live on Earth and ensure that there is always righteousness and prosperity," said the goddesses. "Your desire is my command," said the girl. "But where will I be born on Earth?" she asked.

"You will take birth in the house of Ratnakar and his wife, who are childless. But you must always remember to pray to Lord Vishnu," said the goddesses and vanished after blessing the girl.

As the goddesses had blessed, the girl took birth in the house of Ratnakar. "What a beautiful girl we have

been blessed with," said his wife. "She is like a little flower," said Ratnakar fondling the new born. The couple named the girl Vaishnavi.

Soon the child grew into a very beautiful girl. "Our daughter is not only beautiful, but also more intelligent than her age," said Ratnakar's wife.

"But, have you ever wondered why she is not like other children? She has no desire for toys. She does not play like other children..." added Ratnakar's wife, clearly surprised.

She somehow knew that her daughter was no ordinary child. She was born for a specific purpose.

"Our child is indeed not like other children. But these are the qualities that make her special. I will get the best of teachers for her and make sure that she masters

the Vedas (holy scriptures) and other religious books," replied Ratnakar.

And so began Vaishnavi's education. Her varied interests and curiosity, and her quick understanding

surprised her teachers. However, she was not satisfied with the progress she had made. "I still feel that there is a lot more to learn, Father!" said Vaishnavi.

Ratnakar knew that his daughter was extremely gifted. So he advised her to pray. "Think about the Lord at all times and all your questions will be answered," he told his daughter.

So, while Vaishnavi's friends would be busy playing, she would be busy praying and meditating on the Lord.

Days flew past and the couple knew that soon their daughter would come with a request that they would not be able to refuse. That day came sooner than expected.

"Father, you have looked after my every need. Mother, I am blessed to be born as your child. But the time has come for me to follow the Lord. I need to go to the forest to continue my prayers and meditation," said Vaishnavi.

Ratnakar and his wife were very sad to hear this, but they knew that she was not an ordinary child.

They blessed Vaishnavi and bade her a tearful farewell.

Vaishnavi continued her meditation in the forest. Meanwhile, the kingdom of Ayodhya was brimming with excitement over the crowning of their dear prince Rama. But fate took a different turn, when Kaikeyi asked Dasharatha Lord Rama's father for two

shocking boons. One was to crown her son Bharata as the king of Ayodhya and the second boon was to send Lord Rama on a fourteen-year exile.

The streets of Ayodhya wept as Lord Rama, Sita and Lakshmana left for the forest.

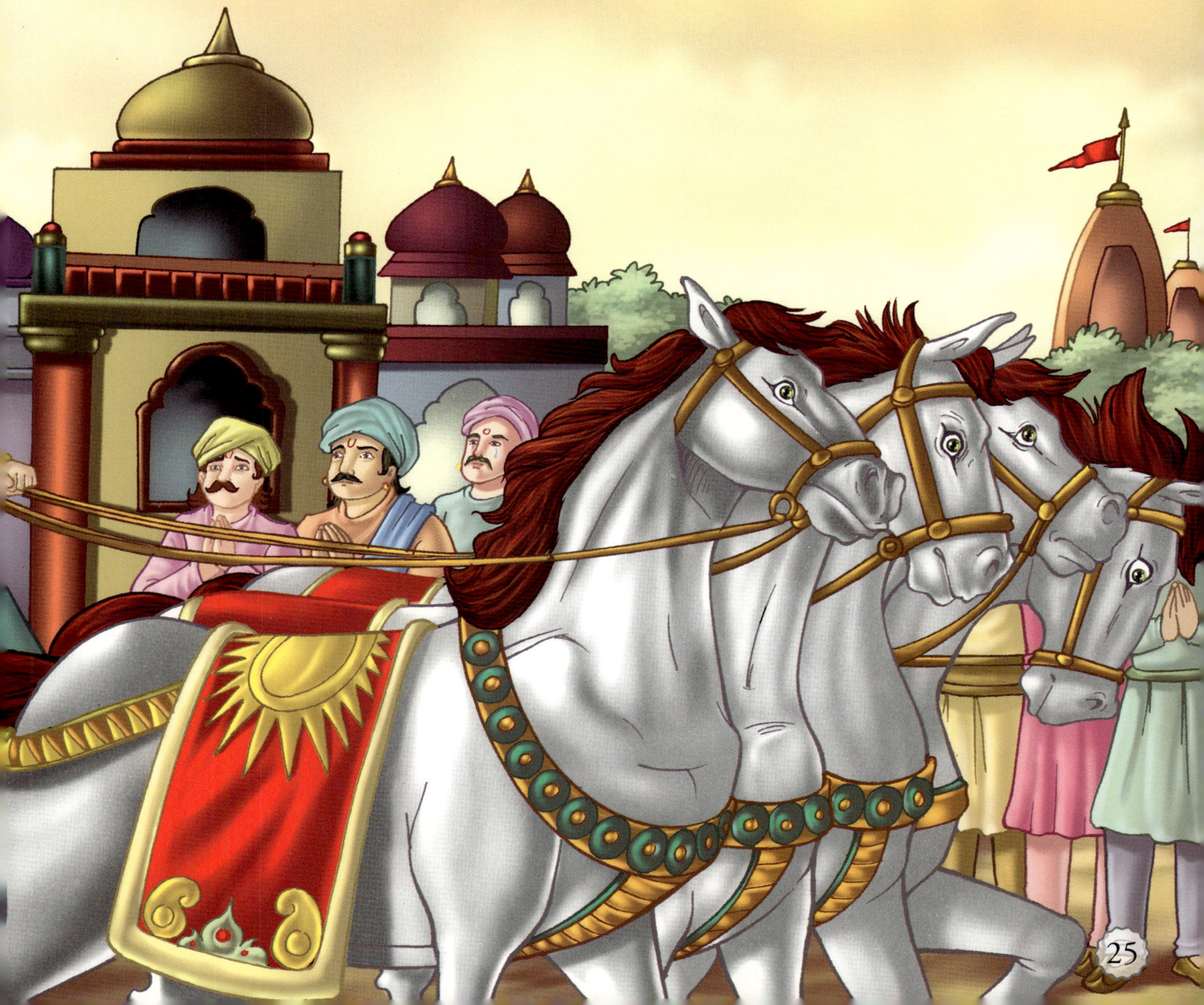

After wandering around the forests for many days, Rama reached the place where Vaishnavi was in deep meditation. Lord Rama's footsteps were instantly recognised by Vaishnavi. "Lord! I cannot believe my eyes. You are already here... Please bless me and take me with you," said Vaishnavi.

"Not now!" replied Lord Rama. "The time has not yet come. I will visit you on my way back from the exile. If you still recognise me, then you will blessed," he said, and left.

Vaishnavi was indeed disappointed. But she did not allow her disappointment to take over what she had set out to achieve. She got back to the prayers that she had been doing. Years passed like this.

By now Lord Rama had killed the evil Ravana and was returning to Ayodhya. But on his way home, he remembered his promise to Vaishnavi. So, he took the form of an old man and decided to meet her. This time, Vaishnavi was unable to recognise him.

"Vaishnavi, look closely," said the old man. It was then that she realised her mistake. "Lord! I lost the

opportunity to be blessed by the one I have been praying to, for the past so many years," she said

tearfully. "All these years have been wasted," said Vaishnavi.

"Do not lose heart!" said Lord Rama. "All is not lost. I will come back to you in my final avtar (incarnation) as Kalki. Then, I will allow you to become a part of me.

Till then, set up an ashram at the foot of the Trikuta hills and bless all the devotees who come to you," said Lord Rama and left for Ayodhya.

Vaishnavi left for northern India. She had to walk through dense forests and thorny

paths. But they did not deter her determination. “Lord Vishnu is my ultimate aim,” she thought to herself

and walked in search of the Trikuta hills. After months of search, she finally found the hills. She set up an ashram (hermitage) at the foothills and began her meditation all over again.

Just like Lord Rama had said, people soon came to know of a girl who had set up a hermitage at the foot of the Trikuta hills. Devotees started flocking to the ashram to seek Vaishnavi's blessings. Months passed and the glory of Ma Vaishnavi spread far and wide.

Meanwhile, not far from the ashram lived an evil hermit called Gorakhnath. Through his divine powers, he came to know of Lord Rama and Vaishnavi's meeting. He called his disciple Bhairavnath to observe Vaishnavi.

"Bhairav, this girl could be our path to becoming the rulers of this world," declared Gorakhnath. "Go and find out more about her," he ordered.

Bhairavnath found the ashram of Vaishnavi very easily. Almost everyone in the area was a devotee of hers. He also found that Vaishnavi carried bow and arrows with her at all times. She always had apes and a ferocious-looking lion with her. He could not believe how beautiful she was till he actually observed her meditating in the ashram.

She is so peaceful, so divine and beautiful, he thought to himself. He wanted to marry Vaishnavi! "Oh lovely one, I wish to marry you," said Bhairavnath to Vaishnavi.

Vaishnavi was shocked by this request. "Go away before you meet your end," ordered Vaishnavi. Bhairavnath was deeply disappointed and left the ashram.

He gave all the information about her to his guru, Gorakhnath.

Meanwhile, in the village near the hills lived an ardent devotee of Ma Vaishnavi, by the name Sridhar. His day would begin

and end with prayers to the Holy Mother. One night, Sridhar had a strange dream. "Conduct a *Bhandara* (community food offering) at your house," said Ma Vaishnavi to him.

Sridhar got up with a jolt. He realised that it was just a dream. But the Holy Mother's orders were sacred to him. *How will I accommodate everyone in this small*

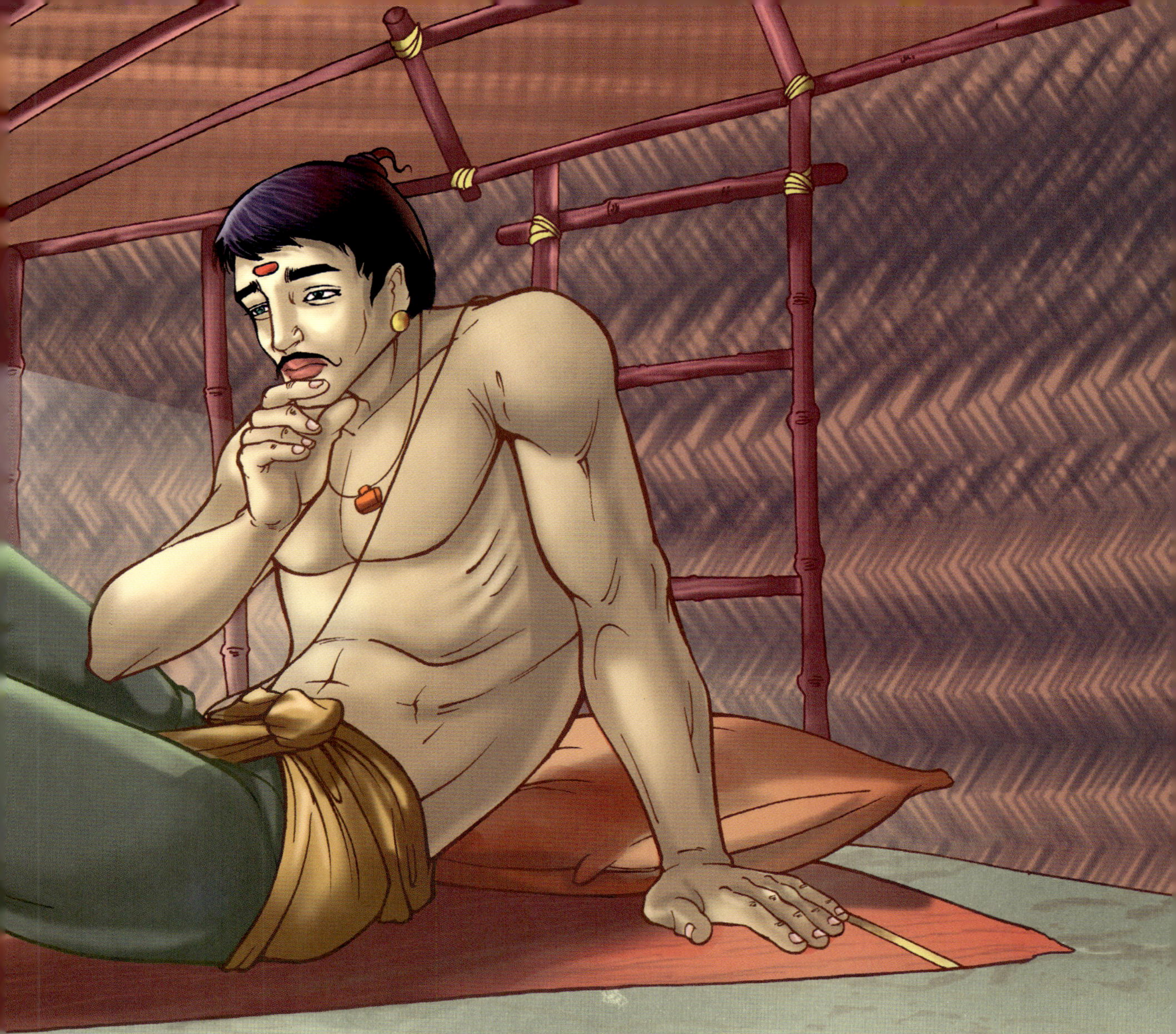

hut, he thought to himself. *And, the groceries – where would they come from?* he wondered.

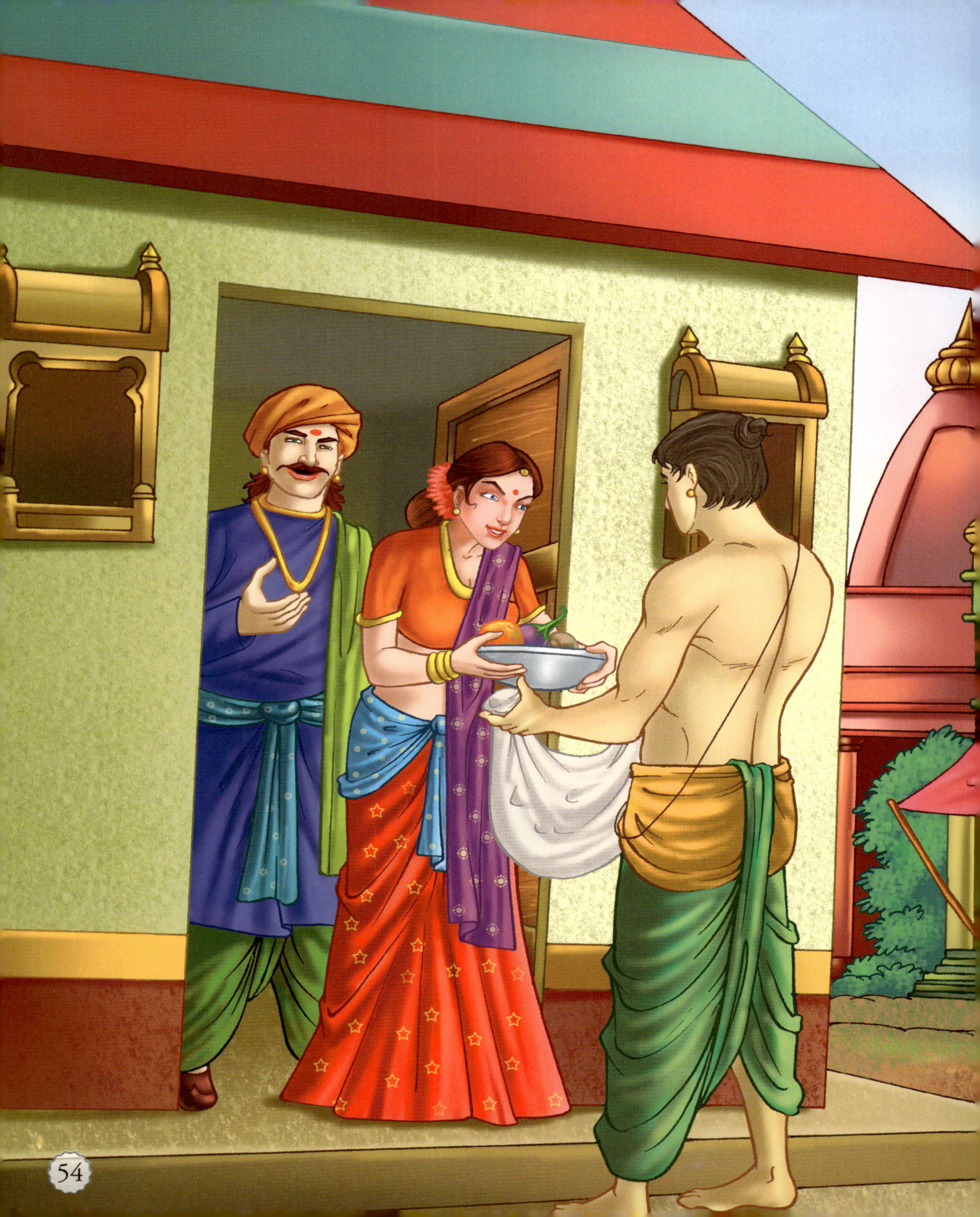

However, he knew that the Holy Mother would not let him down. So he started going from door to door inviting people to his house for the Bhandara. "If you have vegetables or groceries to spare, please give them to me for my Bhandara," requested Sridhar. While

some good people gave him things to use, many turned him down. "How did you have the courage to conduct such a big event at your place, when you don't even

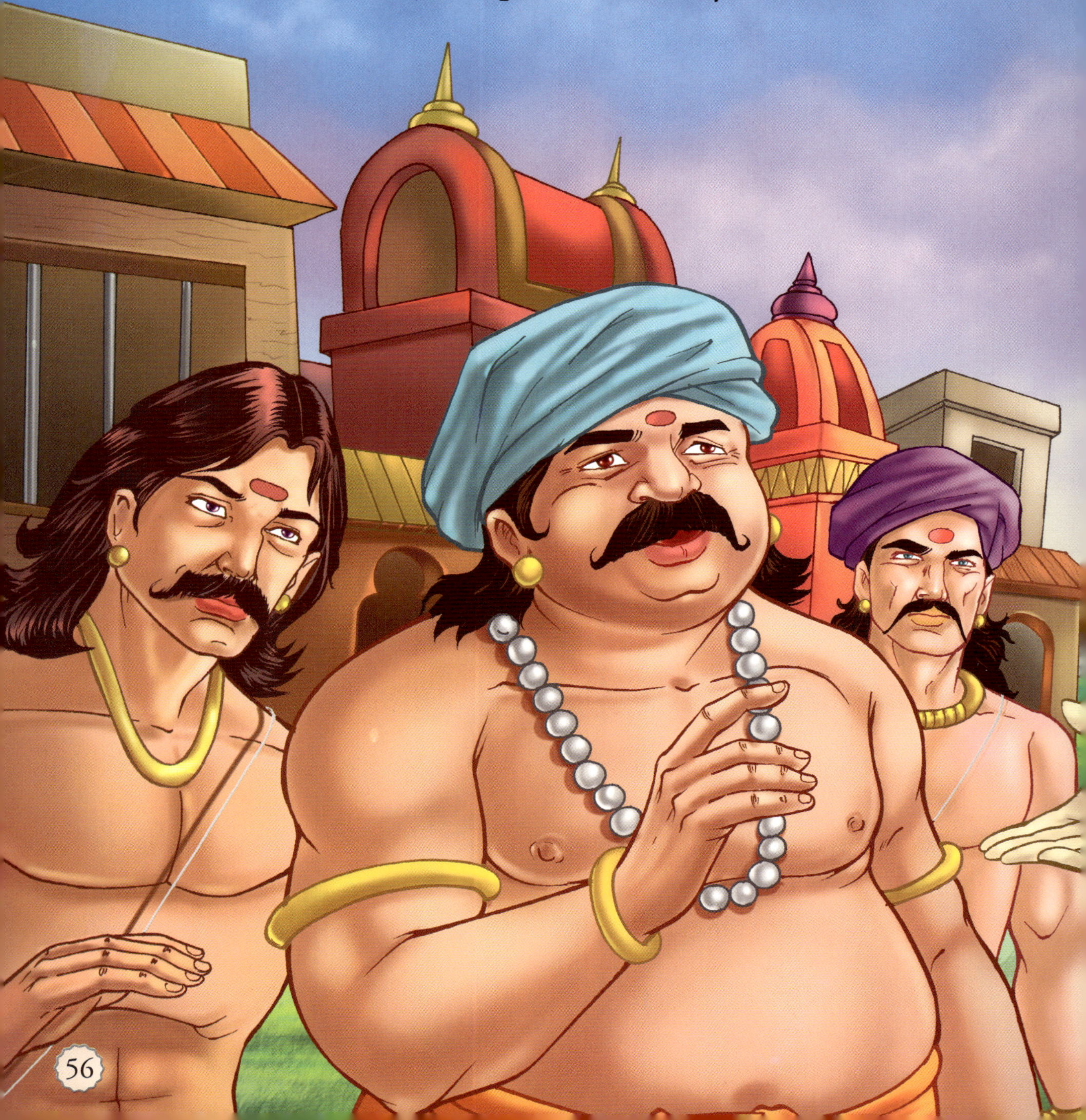

have food to eat yourself?" asked one of his neighbours. But Sridhar did not lose heart.

He even invited Gorakhnath. “We will accept your invitation, but if we are not satisfied with the food,

you will be severely punished," said Gorakhnath. "I have nothing to worry when Ma Vaishnavi is with me," replied Sridhar.

On the night before the Bhandara, Sridhar could not sleep at all. He had spent the entire night wondering how he would feed his guests with the limited groceries he had, and in the limited space he had. Soon, it was day break.

He offered his morning prayers to Ma Vaishnavi and got ready for his Bhandara. The guests started arriving by the afternoon.

The crowd scared Sridhar. But strangely, he could see a miracle happening in front of his eyes. The rooms in his small hut seemed to enlarge, as the number of people increased. There was place for everyone! *Mother, you have come to my rescue,* thought Sridhar. He folded his hands and prayed to her for a few minutes.

Then it was time to serve the guests with the food. This time, Sridhar was not worried, as he knew the Holy Mother would come to his rescue again. He turned

around and saw her seated in the gathering. Sridhar was now assured that no harm would come to him.

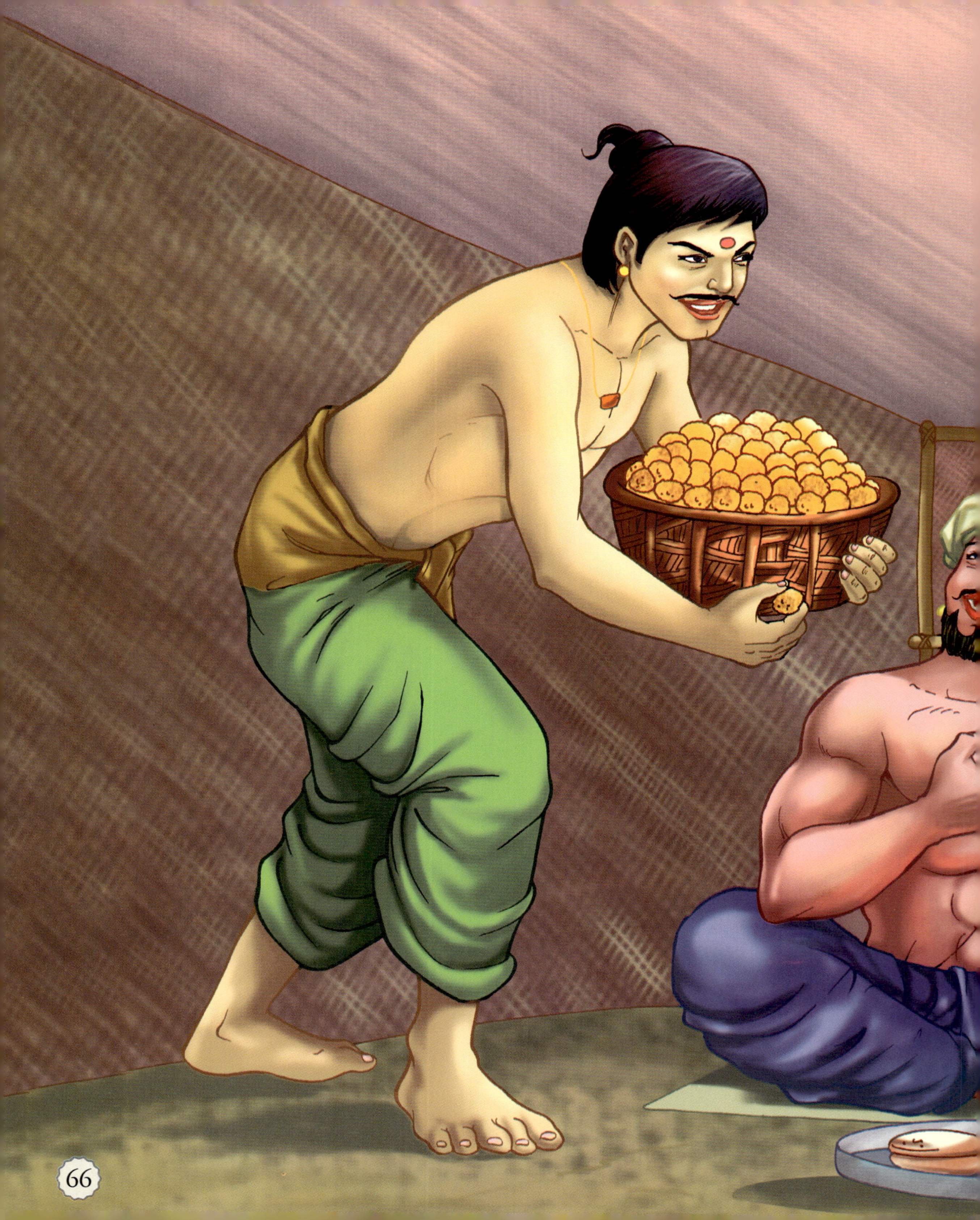

The food seemed to be overflowing. As he served the guests with one dish, more would appear in the vessels on their own. "Sridhar, this is the tastiest food we have ever had," exclaimed everyone in joy. Sridhar was happy to see that he had satisfied everyone and no one had to return hungry.

But Sridhar's choicest guest had still not made his appearance. A few hours after everyone had arrived, Gorakhnath stepped into the hut with his disciples

and Bhairavnath. He saw that countless number of people were stepping out of the hut, and that too after being well-fed.

He looked around and saw that everything was happening in a divine fashion. Meanwhile, Bhairavnath's eyes fell on Vaishnavi. He knew that she was alone, and he was strong in the presence of his guru. So, he made

the mistake of grabbing Vaishnavi's arm. Vaishnavi pushed him aside firmly and started walking towards the mountains. Bhairavnath decided not to leave her

this time, and to chase her to the Trikuta hills. Nine months passed and Bhairavnath could not find

her anywhere in the mountains. One day, he saw her hitting the stone with an arrow, and water gushing out of it. He was curious to know whether she was living in the cave nearby (known as Ardh Kunwaari today). He decided to find out.

On seeing him entering the cave, Vaishnavi tore open a path behind the cave with her trident. "Do not enter this holy cave, Bhairav," ordered Vaishnavi, but Bhairavnath disobeyed her. Finally, Vaishnavi beheaded him.

She severed the head with such force that the head flew and fell on a distant hill top. After his head had been severed, Bhairavnath realised how foolish he had been.

"Oh Holy Mother! Please forgive me," he pleaded. The mother took pity on him and decided to give him a boon. "Every devotee who comes to take my blessings would have to take your blessings after mine. Only then would their journey to Vaishno Devi be complete," blessed Vaishnavi.

"Jai Mata Di"

Then she decided to shed her human form and assumed the face of a rock. She immersed herself into deep meditation.

Ma Vaishnavi today is in the form of a five-and-a half-feet tall rock with three heads (also known as Pindies). The cave is worshipped by one and all as one of the holiest of destinations in India.

OTHER TITLES IN THIS SERIES